1

Young Black Fearless: The 7 Step Guide to Activism

Published by: YBF Publishing, LLC (The Literary Revolutionary) www.theliteraryrevolutionary.com

Copyright © 2016 YBF Publishing, LLC

Manufactured in the United States of America

ISBN-13: 978-1547207077

Learn More about the organizations and coalitions I am involved with, my social justice campaigns and how you can get involved with movement work, visit: www.theliteraryrevolutionary.com

Learn More about the Black Authors Matter campaign, visit: www.blackauthorsmatter.com

Email Me: nia@theliteraryrevolutionary.com

Follow Nia on Social Media: @NiaSadeAkinyemi

YOUNG **BLACK** FEARLESS

The 7 Step Guide to Activism

Written By: Nia Sadé Akinyemi

YBF
PUBLISHING

ATLANTA   MIAMI   NEW YORK   DMV   DALLAS OKC

A Letter from the Author

Since the very first release of this book in November of 2015, I have changed my name. No longer "Walker", I have adopted the surname "Akinyemi" from the Yoruba people of Nigeria, which means, "destined to be a warrior".

As a warrior for my people and a budding scholar of African studies, it was my decision to relinquish the surname given to my people by their owners upon arrival to the Americas, and adopt a traditional African name that I felt was befitting to me, my lineage, and my legacy.

Please note that from this book forward, I will no longer write under the name "Nia Walker", for I have transitioned into another realm of my personal quest of Kujichagulia (self-determination).

Dedication

I dedicate this book to the hundreds of black lives that have been taken by the hands of our enemies.

To Trayvon Martin, Michael Brown Jr., Kendrick Johnson, Tamir Rice, and Jordan Davis

To Sandra Bland, Renisha McBride, Aiyana Stanley-Jones, and Rekia Boyd

To Christopher D. Collins

…and to the countless others who have lost their lives to the trigger fingers of remorseless white cops, racist and hateful white men, and senseless acts of violence among our own.

This is for you.

Acknowledgements

My Son – Each fruit of my labor is for you.

My Love – You have given "team" a whole new meaning.

My Family – This is just the beginning.

My Tribe – Y'all keep me going.

"It is our DUTY to fight for our freedom. It is our duty to WIN. We must LOVE each other and SUPPORT each other. We have NOTHING to lose but our chains." – Queen Assata Shakur

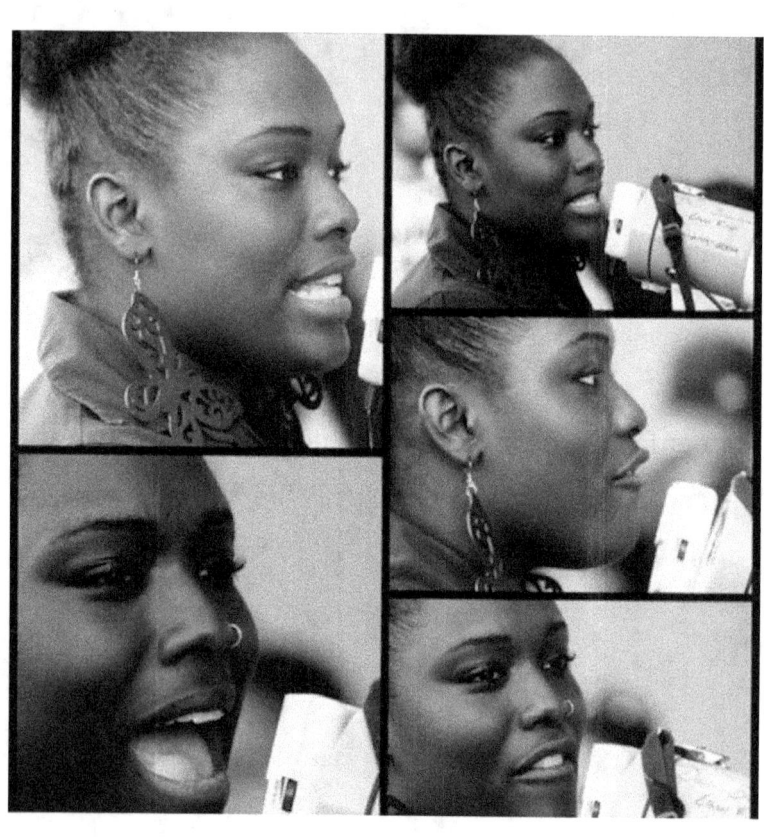

TABLE OF CONTENTS

Foreword

As I sit and ponder the thought of birthing a project so powerful and so magnetic, my insides turn with gratitude. I'm excited about the lives that this project will touch, the change that will come forth, and the healing that will be received - stemming from the depths of the hurt that comes from our past. Our history as black people not only befits who we are today, but it profoundly determines who we'll be tomorrow. We are the future, because we are the foundation. We laid the blueprint for this country. America is ours.

White supremacy has tried to make us believe that by being black, we are to accept injustice and never pursue justice. However, the raw and uncut black history has exemplified that it is simply impossible to merely accept when we were destined to pursue. We were destined to excel. We were destined to reign. For us, acceptance is not a part of our nature. We've always been a people who want and strive for more. We've always worked and aimed for higher. We are a people who are discontent with mediocrity and past generations have proven that to be true.

I would be ashamed to say that the diligence, faith, and strength that made us who we are today is not a success story. I'd be remiss to forget about the blood, sweat, and tears for which we stand on. In their own way, under their own circumstances, in their own capacity, our ancestors were achievers. It is because of them that I am able to write these words today. I feel it would discredit their endurance if we as a people did not continue their legacy by first acknowledging their struggle. The gifts that heaven has instilled in each and every one of its children would not be seen or heard of if it weren't for the strength bestowed upon our people to stand up and fight for our right to live, our right to love, and our right to be black and proud!

I assume because you are reading this book you are either Young and Black in America, know someone who is Young and Black in America, or just want to know what steps to take in becoming ACTIVE while being Young and Black in America. If any of these is the case, be prepared to take notes, as I will discuss the seven steps you need to begin becoming the change you want to see.

In Love & Liberation,
Nia Sadé Akinyemi

Step One: Wake Up!

To Be Young, Black, and Fearless means… To Wake Up and Stay Woke.

For several years, we have witnessed countless acts of unjust violence by whites toward black people. We have been the victims of brutality and unnecessary deaths by the hands of law enforcement. We have cried and mourned the loss of loved ones who were hit by bullets, with and without a name. We have watched as our brothers have been hauled off to serve prison sentences, longer than their age, for minor offenses. We have lost count of the number of times our sisters have been abused, neglected, and left for dead. We have suffered and suffered and suffered some more. We have ached in pain, swallowed our tears, and wallowed in our own blood – sometimes losing hope, but never giving up on the fight for our lives.

Take a minute to think about where you were and how you reacted when you listened to the verdict that George Zimmerman would not be indicted on the murder of Trayvon Martin. Were you upset like me when you found out Michael Dunn shot and killed

Jordan Davis because his music was loud? How did you feel when you saw the footage of Michael Brown's body laying out in the middle of the street in Ferguson? Did you weep for twelve-year-old Tamir Rice when he was killed by police in the park? Did you think for a second that Eric Garner could have been your father? Did you cringe inside when you saw the video of Anthony Hill's naked and unarmed body? How did you feel knowing Freddie Gray died a slow and painful death? Were you outraged when the media tried to convince us that Sandra Bland took her own life? For each of these people – *our* people – named…were you livid? Did you mourn? Were you pissed off? Did you want to fight back in some way? Were you disgusted?

Did you WAKE UP and realize that this is GENOCIDE being handed to us on a blood-stained platter by the servers of white supremacy?

Someone once told me that to be conscious is to live in a constant state of rage. I didn't fully understand what he meant until I temporarily stopped reading the bible and refrained from going to church. After a while, the lack of peace and release became overbearing. It became so draining to be in a constant state of ANGER. Much like Fannie Lou Hamer, *I was sick and tired of being sick and tired.* I am STILL tired every single time I log on to

Facebook, Twitter, or Instagram and see another hashtag for another black body.

For a while, I cried for every life, and then somewhere along the way – after Mike Brown – I grew numb to it. No more tears; no more outrage – just numbness. I felt helpless, and in some ways, I still feel that way. Then I think about GOD and my purpose here on this Earth and I get ANGRY again. But it's that "good" anger. The type of rage that makes me want to go SO HARD for me and my people!

The Charleston shooting in South Carolina at the AME church was the most blatant wake-up call any of us could have had. It was that day that I realized, no matter what, the preservation of my people would always come first. I knew that at that point, if I ever had any doubts about standing up for civil and human rights, those doubts would have to cease. I could never stop the fight for my people, even if I wanted to. It was instilled in me; a seed that had sprouted and could not die. The thing is, many of us have that seed planted within us, and in most cases, that seed has been neglected because of the unfiltered stimulants that have intercepted its growth. Those things of the world that were never truly meant for black people to begin with have stunted the growth of powerful souls: the souls of fighters.

At this point in history, it's really time we as a people stop asking for answers that we already know the answers to. Whether we choose to admit it or not (stay sleep or open our eyes), we know what is REAL and what is FAKE. We know who IS and who ISN'T really for us. Slowly but surely, the monster is awakening. Our voices have been heard and many demands have been made, but still we struggle to find our FOCUS.

Many are AWAKE without any direction. What a time it is to be alive! To be Young, Black, Fearless and to simply FOCUS on US until we have conquered US. The first step is to WAKE UP.

"We have to acknowledge that there are massive problems if we want to facilitate change." – Elaine Brown

Quick Fix:

If you're reading this then chances are you have reached a point where you have become either overwhelmed by the state of America in regards to the brutality against black bodies, or you have become desensitized to it (whether you have chosen to or not).

TODAY:

Take a moment out of your busy schedule to meditate on the country's current state. All you should need is about 30 minutes away from the Internet, social media sites, news outlets, and any other distractions you may have. Give yourself an opportunity to reflect on the long list of names of those individuals who were shot and killed while unarmed. Say their names. Go and listen to Janelle Monae and the Wondaland Team's "Hell You Talmbout." Imagine, just for a second, that those names belonged to your mother, your father, your sister, your brother, your cousin, your best friend, or your child. Give yourself a minute to grieve for those black bodies.

Are you WOKE?

Use these next few pages to write down your thoughts. How do you feel about the current state of America as it pertains to the injustice and genocide against black and brown lives?

_____

_____

_____

_____

_____

_____

_____

_____

_____

_____

_____

_____

_____

_____

_____

_____

Step Two: Don't Talk About It | Be About It

To be young, black, and fearless means to walk the walk FIRST… then let your actions speak for you.

I have this problem with my people who always have a mouthful to say on Facebook, Instagram, Twitter, Periscope, and whatever other social media outlet you can think of, but don't have a mere SLIP of a receipt to indicate what they actually do to help a given situation. With all that is going on in America and in the world today, there is little need for any more people on the internet whining and complaining about what's wrong with the world, if they are not actually doing anything to transform the world.

I get it. Change rarely ever happens overnight. Sometimes it takes months, and even years, to come up with solutions to critical problems, such as the issue of race in America. What I personally have developed a problem with is when individuals who have never proposed a plan of action or attempted to bring forth a solution have ill regards for the person who has. There is an extremely thin line between conscious individuals who put in WORK for the black community and those who simply work their FINGERS on keyboards for heated Facebook debates, having absolutely no record of their contribution to the community. For those individuals, I have one simple request: *Bruh. Have a seat.* Going off on social media about what NEEDS to be done within the black community or in response to the brutalization towards black bodies means absolutely NOTHING if that pop off is not backed by real action. Hence, why my second tip is to buck the system – in real life!

We live in the day and age of high thriving technology. We are able to pretty much do everything we can imagine with the pretty little phone sitting in the palm of our hands. It has become so easy for us to express our deep sadness and vent our greatest angers. It has allowed us to be able to post injustice and talk about it for days by commenting on videos, photos, and memes, yet has handicapped us to the point where we think that we have done enough!

How much more does it take for us to realize that in order to make change happen, we actually have to get off of social media and do something about it? Do they have to come kill one of our family members for us to realize that this isn't a joke, or do we just continue to give our emotional, philosophical, psychological, and theological analysis on the state of America via 140 characters, hoping that the world will implement the plan overnight?

I am one to talk because just less than a year ago, I would be the one on social media igniting fires with my words about inherent racism and about what we weren't doing right as a community. All of that talk quickly came to an end when I began to actually get involved with local justice-seeking organizations, in which I was then able to take all of that built up, angry energy and put it in the right direction. I was finally learning to minimize my rants and actually facilitate change.

Are you a talker or a doer?

Earlier this summer, I made a YouTube video to talk about the different type of "critics" of both "the system" and of the black community. I was so sick of reading everyone's posts about how upset they were with certain issues, but anytime I invited them out to do the work, they were either scared or wouldn't make the time for it. Needless to say, I realized that unless something tragic happens to them on a more personal level, the likelihood of them wanting to stand up for someone else is slim until you challenge their ego and credibility.

For every critic who feels the need to comment, criticize or complain about anything you either don't understand or think you can do better, ask yourself this question: *"What can I do to make the situation better OTHER than running my mouth?"* If you cannot answer this question, you are most likely a part of the problem.

"I'm the biggest hypocrite of 2015. When I finish this if you listening, I'm sure you will agree. This plot is bigger than me, its generational hatred. It's genocism, it's grimy, little justification." – Kendrick Lamar, "The Blacker the Berry" (2015)

Quick Fix:

Stop complaining and ranting on social media outlets about the problems we face. Instead, find a solution to those problems. That solution could mean implementing a plan of action within our schools, helping out at the local recreation center or homeless shelter in our community, rallying in front of courthouses where a grand jury will be held, running for local office, or holding a community forum to discuss other ways for everyone to create a better livelihood. If you are really about what you say... I mean REALLY about it... DON'T just talk about it. BE about it.

"The ultimate measure of a man is not where he stands in moments of comfort and convenience, but where he stands at times of challenge and controversy." – Martin Luther King, Jr.

TODAY:

Log off from your Facebook, Twitter, Instagram, Periscope, Snapchat, or whatever other social media site that you would have otherwise ranted on about how you feel regarding the treatment of black people vs. white privilege. That long and elaborated status you were going to post, that 140 character tweet you were getting ready to send, and that super deep meme you were going to repost – write it down on paper. Look at it. Study it. Ask yourself, *"Is there a solution to the problem in this post I was about to make?"* If there is, good.

Write down how you are going to implement that solution. Once you do that, list the resources you will need for this plan to be successful. Do you need money, time, or people power? Will you need approval from elected officials or is this something the community can manage on its own?

Now, if the elaborated status update; tweet; or meme you wrote down does not have a careful plan to create a solution, THIS is your opportunity to create that plan. Look at the paper and map it out. Ask yourself these questions: *"How can I implement this plan? What resources will it take me to effectively execute this plan?"*

In the most heartfelt manner, I have to ask that we as a people do the work instead of talk about what work needs to be done. Then, even after doing the work, we must utilize the camera and video upload buttons. It's imperative to SHOW the people what work you are doing in the community rather than simply TELLING them what they need to do. From my experience, I have learned that no matter how much work you put into a status or post, the REAL differences are made when you SHOW people the work and then ENCOURAGE them to join you.

I remember the days when I would go on and on about how black people needed to rebel against the institutions of racism. I would MAYBE get about 20-30 likes on average of people who MIGHT have agreed with what I said. It wasn't until I began my activist diary on my Facebook that people actually started paying closer attention to my efforts toward creating a better future. Those 20-30 likes of agreement turned into 30-40 inbox messages, comments, calls, and texts asking how they could get involved. At that point, I saw that being about the WORK for the community and not a part of the NEGATIVE OPINIONS of the community is what gave me that leverage of people power, energy, and resources I needed to build and grow within the movement.

"You are either part of the solution or part of the problem." –
Eldridge Cleaver

Let's write out a plan. How can you do to be the change you wish to see in the world?

_____

_____

_____

_____

_____

_____

_____

_____

_____

_____

_____

_____

_____

_____

_____

_____

Step Three: Know Your Role | Play Your Role

To be young, black, and fearless means to know your role in the revolution, and then play that role.

Everyone cannot be on the front lines of the revolution. However, everyone CAN do the grassroots work. It is all about utilizing your strengths for the greater good of the community.

My grassroots efforts began during my encounter with my local NAACP chapter: the Clayton County NAACP Branch. When I reached out to Madame President Baldwin, I was only hoping to acquire an internship position with the branch in an effort to complete my requirements for graduation from Clayton State University. I honestly had no idea that this internship would change my life and change my views on life the way that it did. After becoming involved in an organization with such a rich history rooted and embedded in the movement for civil and human rights, it was only right for me to feel at home. Ever since I was a child, I had been yearning to be a part of something bigger and greater than me that would create and implement levels of change that would end up in history books. That happened for me when I began to learn the business of movement work and started networking and making major connections that turned into very essential relationships.

My first induction to grassroots movement work began on the case of Dhoruba Bin-Wahad. As I began my internship with the NAACP, I became aware that our organization had joined a newly formed coalition: The Coalition for Justice and Police Accountability. This coalition was formed to be the leading force of people power for Baba Dhoruba's fight for justice, as he had been assaulted and brutalized by a Clayton County, Georgia (now former) police officer, Ryan Hall. Dhoruba was 69 years old, moving into his new home in Clayton County, when neighbors called the police, suspecting there was a break in. When the officers got to Baba Dhoruba's home, instead of asking questions first, they manhandled him to the ground, slamming his head into the brick wall of his own home while forcing handcuffs on him and ordering him to sit on the front steps of his home like a criminal. As graphic as the altercation was and having been caught on camera by the neighbors across the street, I am thankful that the situation did not escalate, becoming another story of an unarmed man being shot to death by the police. Furthermore, the officers picked the RIGHT one to assault. Little did they know, Dhrouba was a former Black Panther and had spent 19 years in the penitentiary as a Political Prisoner.

As a member of the Coalition, it took a while for me to figure out what my role was in this movement. The ultimate goal of the case of Wahad was to bring an indictment on the police officer who assaulted our elder. This push for an indictment was spearheaded by the prominent law firm in the area known to handle such cases of police brutality, hate crimes, and social injustices. In addition, there were local faith leaders and even a church who took a stand in the push. Organizations all over Atlanta area's community joined forces in an effort to fight for justice and we did so by staying up ALL NIGHT on the courthouse steps the night before the grand jury's hearing.

So where did I fit in?

As I stated before, my initial introduction to the grassroots movement was through my internship. However, as I began to learn about the organizations involved in the coalition and get my feet wet by making connections, I realized my strength. I was so

EXCITED to finally be ACTIVELY fighting for justice. In my excitement, I wanted to talk about what demonstrations were coming up and make sure everyone was always all on one accord. What I found is that in my need to plan, discuss, and execute every step needed to make this move successful, I turned out to be the ultimate organizer.

I found my role.

For years I thought that to be "down" with the revolution meant being on the front lines at all the marches, protests, and demonstrations. Though being there is essential and profound, it is not the ONLY way to contribute to the revolution. There are so many roles that everyone can uphold which play an important part in making any demonstration a success.

When I first began organizing rallies for social justice and reform, I would often get upset when people did not answer my plea for showing up. I felt like if you are black in America and you don't live under a rock, then surely you are as upset and outraged as I am about the current state and mistreatment of black people. I wanted so badly for people to just come and fight with the masses, because I just knew that those individuals would be full of the drive like I had been. What I didn't realize is that many are not "scared" like I had once assumed. In fact, many people want to be a part of the movement but just don't know HOW.

It is so extremely important for rising activists to identify their role as it pertains to the movement for social justice and change and do the work of that role. For clarity, let me give a few examples of how each occupation could add to a protest, sit-in, rally, or any other demonstration.

The Attorneys use their legal expertise to work on building the cases and presenting them in court.

The Pastors and Church Members pray and fast for our victories.

The Graphic Designers create our flyers for events.

The Teachers gather up students and young people to come out and experience the movement and make signs to carry for marches and/or media.

The Community Affairs Directors make sure the logistics, such as time and location (whether property is public or private), are appropriate for demonstrations.

The Promoters use their internet following and connections to spread the word.

The Artists bring their gifts and talents to the demonstrations and they speak on the movement through their art, both visually and musically.

The Reporters make sure that accurate stories are given to the media and highlight, at all costs, the positive engagement throughout the black community.

The Journalists and Bloggers create a track record of movement events by writing about every demonstration that takes place in the words of our own and not leaving it in the hands of the shady media.

The Public Speakers give moving, empowering, and motivating speeches in order to keep the spirit of justice high in the air.

The Police Officers, who are actually DOWN with the movement, show up at the rallies in order to assure our safety.

The Law School Students make sure that every action we take is legal and safe.

The College Students provide their fiery energy and are ready to fight!

The Professors and Historians are there to keep us educated on the history of and tactics used in successful grassroots movement work.

The Doctors and Nurses are there to be on call in case anyone gets hurt or gets sick.

The Hospitality People are there to make sure demonstrators have water, food, fans, napkins, bug spray, or WHATEVER is needed to be comfortable while doing movement work.

The Kids are there as a reminder that every move we make is with them in mind because they are the next generation.

For every person, every occupation, every service, and every area of expertise – there is a job to do. Many people are unaware that they can be ACTIVE on account of these very roles. Showing up at a demonstration is not pointless and it is not frightening when you know the role that you play.

"I decided to teach because I think that any person who studies philosophy has to be involved actively." – Angela Davis

Quick Fix:

Find out what your role is in the revolution and in demonstrations that are held. Once you know what your role is, play your role and encourage others to do the same.

TODAY:

Write down the top three things that you are best at doing. After you identify those three things, write down three things you could do to utilize those skills within the revolution. Here is my personal list as an example:

What Am I Good At?	How Can I Utilize This Skill?
• I am a skilled vocalist. • I am an excellent writer. • I am a proficient organizer and teacher.	• I can use my voice to sing uplifting songs to encourage the community. • I can create a journal and blog about every demonstration I attend in order to encourage more people to get involved in the fight for justice. • I can organize events and raise awareness by teaching the community about things that are going on around us.

When you have successfully identified the three things you do best, you can either find an organization that represents the changes you wish to implement, or create one. I recommend forming alliances and starting coalitions with similar agendas because it is a proven fact that there is power in numbers.

Write it down. What is it that you are good at, or that you have access to where you can utilize it within the movement? How?

_____

_____

_____

_____

_____

_____

_____

_____

_____

_____

_____

_____

_____

_____

_____

Step Four: Educate Yourself & Prepare the Next Generation

To be young, black, and fearless means to first educate yourself on studies concerning black people in order to educate the masses.

There is a popular saying that goes, "Knowledge is power." There is another saying that poses a challenge to the prior that says, "Knowledge is power only if it is applied." The latter quote to me is very important because, if you really think about it, it makes the most sense. Anyone can know every little intricate detail about something and not do anything about it. Sometimes we're lucky if that person even knows what to do about it.

When you make the decision to step up your game and present yourself to the world as a young and black trailblazer, you have to have some type of knowledge and awareness of what you're getting yourself into. Knowledge of self, of your history, and of the greats that paved the way before you is what yields you longevity in this movement.

"A people without the knowledge of their past history, origin and culture is like a tree without roots." – Marcus Garvey

Let's be honest. Let's get real. At this point in history, as young black people in America, we are aware – or at least should be aware – of how messed up the public school system's curriculum is when it comes to teaching African American History. An old high school teammate of mine posted a picture of a PowerPoint slide one of her professors had shown in a lecture not too long ago. It read, "White privilege is your history being a part of the core curriculum and mine only being taught as an elective." When I first saw the post, my mouth dropped on the spot. It didn't necessarily catch me off guard, and it wasn't something I didn't already know, but what got me was that the way in which it was stated. It was probably the REALEST it could have EVER been said and I was at a loss for words. It was like the words I had been looking for to describe the lack of information was revealed right before my eyes and I couldn't believe I hadn't analyzed and reiterated it like that myself!

In a complex sentence, many young people of African descent are reminded that when it comes to our history, we are at not the priority. It amazed me when I saw President Barack

Obama's election in the 2010 social studies books. I thought that was extremely fast! What didn't surprise me though was that Obama's election pages (in the history book) came about three or four pages after those about Martin Luther King Jr. and Rosa Parks. Then, of course, when Obama's chapter was covered, that was it for the black history lesson. Oh, and let me not forget to mention that the "black history" text is almost ALWAYS in the very back of the book, which I believe is on purpose because teachers very rarely get to the final chapters of the history books before the school year is over. Some could say it is all a setup, while I think it's just a strategic move, because the reality is that the creators of these American History textbooks are almost ALWAYS white and they probably know no more of the truth than we've been taught.

African American Studies courses in undergrad is what changed my ENTIRE perspective on being black in America. In these classes, I had the pleasure of being introduced to not just the black life in America, but black life across the entire Afrikan diaspora. My love and appreciation for who I am and where I stand as a black woman grew to another level as I sat in courses such as: African American Literature, Caribbean Literature, African American Studies, Africana Woman Studies, and the Psychology of the African American Experience. It was in these courses that my thirst and hunger for knowledge was at an all-time high. I must admit, I probably never read an entire book throughout my college years that DIDN'T come from an AFAM (African American Studies) course.

"The revolution has always been in the hands of the young. The young always inherit the revolution." – Huey P. Newton

In all honesty, the revolutionary spirit I carry is one that is deeply rooted and has been within me since my childhood days. My parents were always revolutionary in their own way; my daddy specifically was a bit of a radical. I read *The Autobiography of Malcolm X* when I was in the fifth grade and Huey P. Newton's *Revolutionary Suicide* by the time I was in eighth grade. I could tell you left and right, back and forth, the names; missions; and purpose of each legendary African American who stepped foot on American soil. Yet, I didn't know much about pre-slavery (like most of us), and I still learned the bad habit of blaming everything on "the white man."

Now, don't get me wrong; I understand much more now the analogy of "the white man" and how deep the scars of institutionalized racism has cut black people. However, as I increase in my knowledge and awareness of successful movements that took place in the past, I am able to focus more now on MY people than worrying too much about what white people have done to try and break us.

Everyone reading this text may not have come from a background that encouraged the study of black life, black struggles, and black victories, but whether you've come from that type of background or not, there are endless opportunities to learn about these things. When you are contemplating how you are going to make a difference in a country that is embedded in institutionalized racism, who still believes in oppressing the black race, and who still makes excuses for why ALL LIVES DON'T MATTER, it is THAT much more important for you to get to know the truth. We live in a time now that the Internet can link us to whatever book, program, or person we need to retrieve the knowledge and understanding of black life in America at any point. It is simply up to us to take advantage of the opportunities and use them to build a platform so that we can successfully edify the black community, tear down the barriers of white supremacy, and ultimately, become a world changer.

"Once Kings, now we're pawns in this chess game. Wall Street got black slave blood stains, which means, we built this city and never got scraps, while the devil got fat."
– J. Cole, New York Times (2013)

Quick Fix:

If you feel like the public school system failed you in any aspect, do what you have to do in order to educate yourself. Study Malcolm X. His greatest education came from within the walls of prison. He sought the knowledge he missed in grade school BY ANY MEANS NECESSARY and he went on to be one of the most profound leaders of the Civil Rights Movement.

Below I have listed a number of books that every rising activist and community organizer should have on their "Reading To-Do List," as well as a number of current documentaries, public figures, and organizations that are teaching the information needed to be successful in movement work and ultimate change.

Try and read a new book from this list at least every two weeks or once a month, whichever fits your schedule. Follow the Instagram Pages listed and check out the corresponding websites and blogs. And, if you haven't already, watch *Hidden Colors* 1, 2, and 3.

Books/Texts/Documentaries:

The Autobiography of Malcolm X (By: Alex Haley)

Revolutionary Suicide (By: Huey P. Newton)

"Letter from Birmingham Jail" (By: Dr. Martin Luther King Jr.)

The African Unconscious (By: Edward Bynum)

The Bible (Specifically with the understanding of Revolutionary Jesus)

We Will Shoot Back (By: Dr. Akinyele Umoja)

The Mis-education of the Negro (By: Carter G. Woodson)

A Taste of Power (By: Elaine Brown)

Class Struggle in Africa (By: Kwame Nkrumah)

Capitalism and Slavery (By: Eric Williams)

Blood in My Eyes (By: George Jackson)

Seat of the Soul (By: Gary Zukav)

Assata: An Autobiography (By: Assata Shakur)

The New Jim Crow (By: Michelle Alexander)

The Souls of Black Folk (By: W.E.B Dubois)

Blueprint for Black Power (By: Amos Wilson)

100 Lynchings (By: Ralph Ginzberg)

Elementary Genocide 1 & 2 (Produced By: Raheim Shabazz)

Hidden Colors (Directed By: Tariq Nasheed)

Slavery By Another Name (Both Book & Film)

People & Pages to Follow on Social Media:

African Unification

Sancopha League

The Root

Dr. Umar Johnson

Afrikan Library

PanAfrikanBooklist

TODAY:

Read a book. Find a group of kids (other than your own) and teach them something. Obtaining all of this information about our history and our rich culture will be in vain if you don't spread that knowledge to those coming after you. We are the NOW generation preparing the way for the NEXT generation, and it is our duty to train them up. Furthermore, sometimes on this road to consciousness and activism, we can lose our faith when trying to convince older people that the system is corrupt. On the other hand, it is not that difficult to teach kids how to overcome the barriers that have been set in place.

"It is easier to build up children, than to repair broken men."
– Frederick Douglass

Write it down. Choose a text or documentary listed above and use this space to jot down notes that will help you further yourself as an activist.

_____

_____

_____

_____

_____

_____

_____

_____

_____

_____

_____

_____

_____

_____

_____

_____

Step Five: Organize and Document

To be young, black, and fearless means to organize effective demonstrations that create long-lasting change and document every step of the way.

One of the most important things you can do when making the decision to become active in the community is to associate yourself with an organization that is doing the work you wish to do. Like I mentioned in Step Three, you have to know your role, learn your role, and then play your role. Not everyone is an organizer, but that doesn't mean that they cannot be a part of a major organization. In fact, if you know that you are not one who is good with planning and organizing but you have the spirit to serve the people, then it would behoove you to join an already existing organization. Joining forces with an already established organization with like-minded views will align you with the right tribe to build and grow with. You will then be in a better position to implement positive agendas and overall greatness.

For example, if I were just getting started in the activist game and considering my current profession as an educator, I would search for a local organization that caters to education. It could be as specific as after school tutoring and mentoring or be as upfront as joining the campaign of a candidate for school board.

When it comes to orchestrating a major demonstration, much like the #UpAllNight move that my coalition did for Dhoruba Bin-Wahad; the various #BlackLivesMatter campaigns and protests across the country; or even Minister Louis Farrakhan's #JusticeOrElse march, organizing is CRUCIAL. It takes a lot of hard work and effort to pull off such major movements, and often times, egos can collide. What we have to keep in mind when we are organizing these demonstrations is that it is all so much bigger than us. We have to be mindful of the lives that have been lost and why we're doing the work in the first place. We have to encourage individuals to be the standard; to show up and just stand if that is all they can do. There is SO MUCH POWER in NUMBERS!

One man or woman can have the wisdom and insight to lead a nation, but without the people, the movement fails. When joining alliances across organizational and political lines, you are saying to yourself and to the people that we are in this together, whether we get along or not, whether our views are the same or not – we choose unity.

I had the best time of my life on the lawn of the Nation's Capital on October 10, 2015! There is absolutely nothing that can be said and no one in this world who can ever take away the feeling that myself and many other people had on that day as we stood together in unity and in solidarity. For me, 10/10/15 was like a family reunion! I hugged so many people I never knew and called more people "sister and brother" than I ever have in my life. It was truly AMAZING and INSPIRING to know that we actually do have a leader who is alive and well that made that happen.

From an organizer's viewpoint, I learned so much. One of the most important things I was able to grasp from the march was that again, THERE IS POWER IN OUR NUMBER! So what if the major media and news stations didn't come to highlight that vast amount of melanin in one area for the world to see! At that point, most of us out there didn't even CARE! We were there and no media showed, which made it all so very clear. It became OUR duty to document EVERY thing we witnessed on that day. We were the media. That day, many of us for the first time became journalists, photographers, and personalities! It came with the territory of being black and proud, putting egos aside, and being the change we wanted to see.

"Black leadership has to recognize that principles more than speech, character more than a claim, is greater in advancing the cause of our liberation than what has transpired thus far."
– Louis Farrakhan

Quick Fix:

No matter how big, small, biased, or political a demonstration may be, understanding the power of numbers is enough to have us backing and supporting one another. There have been rallies that I have worked on with some interesting people. There have been times when I started out as a lead organizer and I had to take the back seat because of the politics that may have come into play. There has never been a time, though, where I turned my back on one of my beloved movement family members, because I know the power that number has. Chains literally BREAK when we show up in numbers. It's all about organizing and documenting.

TODAY:

Write down this affirmation and speak it daily. Use it as your reminder that unity within our community is the most effective way to create change.

Affirmation:

I am so grateful and proud to know that through my diligence in community organizing, adding my body to the people power, and constantly documenting the good, great, bad, and ugly of this movement – change has really come.

Write it down. Think of this space as the beginning manuscript of YOUR book. Remember, history doesn't write itself. It's up to us to tell OUR story. When you've finished your first two chapters, email me so we can get it published! ybfpublishing@gmail.com

_____

_____

_____

_____

_____

_____

_____

_____

_____

_____

_____

_____

_____

_____

_____

Step Six: Vote Anyway

To be young, black, and fearless means to exercise your right to vote even when you don't think it will make much of a difference; you do it anyway.

Voting should not be one's ONLY answer to the revolution of societal change; however, it DOES hold great weight and is extremely important. In my opinion, one of the greatest accomplishments we have made as a people was successfully fighting for and winning the right to vote. Going way back to slavery when black people were considered to be only 3/5ths of a person, to the 1860's passing of the Voting Rights Act, to almost 100 years later on Bloody Sunday in Selma, Alabama, our ancestors never gave up the fight to retrieve those rights no matter how long it took. Personally, that is enough for me to get up and vote during election season. I am big on making sure that our ancestors' hard work does not go in vain. I always think back to the blood, sweat, and tears that went into making the black vote count. Choosing not to honor that sacrifice is blasphemous, and is not an option. However, I do understand that there are quite a few of us YOUNG black bodies in America that seem to think that voting is unnecessary.

For those of my people who fail to understand the objective and power of voting... Let me give you a better idea.

The objective is to vote in OUR people!

Our job is to VOTE our people into positions of power. Not just black people, but good black people who will work toward making sure the community receives the absolute best. More importantly, putting these individuals into positions that affect our livelihood on a more personal level is what creates societal change. It is more important at this point in American history to have more black elected officials in our own neighborhoods than to have a Black President.

No, I am not throwing an ounce of shade to President Obama, because I love and have great respect for him. I am simply stating the obvious. There are positions that hit closer to home.

This is how we win:

(1)   By voting in more Black Judges to be in charge of sentencing Black People according to the actual crime they commit (and give the reasonable time due) and not according to their black skin that is seen as a threat to society. Think about it. If we had more black judges in office like Judge Olu Stevens from Louisville, Kentucky who just recently dismissed a jury for not having enough black jurors, wouldn't we see more JUSTICE in the courtrooms?

(2)   By voting in more Black District Attorneys to be in charge of prosecuting Police Officers who break laws, violate codes of ethic, and use their badge as a weapon to wrongfully profile and/or brutalize community members who do nothing more than be "of color." We can really stop right here. At least 50% of the cases dealing with police brutality and wrongful deaths on ALL the names we've had to say #JusticeFor_____, would have led to indictments if the District Attorneys on these cases

were conscious Blacks. Don't we want to see that type of shift in the judicial system?

(3)   By voting in more Black State Representatives into the House and Senate to make sure that old laws are amended, unjust laws are removed, and new laws are created to hold people accountable for situations regarding, standing your ground, gun laws, etc.

(4)   By voting in more Black School Board Members to make sure that our children are receiving the best quality education and are not being overlooked and left behind or pushed ahead when they are not academically ready. Also, to make sure that the educators who teach our children are taken care of (financially) so that they will effectively and HAPPILY take care of our youth.

(5)   By voting in more Black City Council Members, Commissioners, and Mayors that will fight for, make and fulfill commitments for, and provide opportunities for their constituents.

The objective is not to vote, but to VOTE BLACK and then hold our elected officials ACCOUNTABLE for our well-being. Just as easily as we can vote these officials into office, we can gather the people power to vote them out in the event that they fail to do their jobs.

If you're really down for being socially conscious...
If you're really down for the revolution...
If you really want to fight systematic oppression...
If you really want to honor our ancestors....

NOT Voting is NOT the Answer.....But **Voting BLACK is**!

Quick Fix:

If you are NOT registered to vote and would like to register, visit your local NAACP office or DMV and request registration to vote. If you live in the state of Georgia, visit https://registertovote.sos.ga.gov/GAOLVR/welcome.do#no-back-button and register online NOW!

Today:

If you are registered to vote, I encourage you to find local black candidates that you truly believe in, that stand for what is right, and that do not neglect the black community – stand with them! Support them! Campaign for them! Then, if you are not in an area where there are any of our people running for an office and you KNOW or FEEL you can do the job – RUN FOR IT! ***To be young, black, and fearless means to GO FOR IT… even when you are in doubt or are afraid.*** This is one of the biggest lessons that I learned as I campaigned to become the Commissioner in my county's district.

Also, don't let age discourage you. When I ran for Commissioner of my district, I will made history as the youngest to ever run for that position in the entire state of Georgia, at age 22. That's a proud moment in itself, because as I document my own history and teach the youth how to document as well, I can guarantee that I will end up in the American History books and African Studies courses.

Quick Facts:

- Young, Black, and Fearless **Jasmine Twitty** became the youngest judge in the history of Easley, South Carolina at 25 years old.

- Young, Black, and Fearless **Michael Tubbs** became the youngest City Councilman to be elected in Stockton, California at 22 years old.

- Young, Black, and Fearless **Mary Sheffield** became the youngest City Councilwoman to be elected in Detroit, Michigan at 26 years old.

- Young, Black, and Fearless **Jewell Jones** just became the youngest elected City Councilman to be elected in Inkster, Michigan at 20 years old – just last month in November 2015!

- Young, Black, and Fearless SISTERS **Misskeith and Markeita Prevost** both ran for seats in the Louisiana House of Representatives this year. Though both sisters lost, they made history as the first two BLACK sisters to enter the Louisiana House of Representatives race, and Misskeith made history by becoming the YOUNGEST to run at 20 years old.

Write it down. What does having the right to vote mean to you?

_____

_____

_____

_____

_____

_____

_____

_____

_____

_____

_____

_____

_____

_____

_____

_____

_____

_____

Step Seven: Be Bold | Be Fearless | Be Unapologetic

To be young, black, and fearless means to be bold and unapologetic in all things concerning our people.

This last step to activism is probably the easiest yet, but sometimes it can prove to be the most challenging to conquer for more reasons than one. When you come from where we come from, the great Mama Africa, rich from the blood of warriors, it would seem as though this step would be a breeze. But, when you come from where we come from, robbed of our homeland; sold into slavery; beaten; raped; murdered; left for dead; and ultimately, psychologically damaged for years to come, you can understand why this may be a challenge. But it's not something we cannot overcome, for we have overcome years of what we were told would be the death of us.

"A man is either free or he is not. There cannot be any apprenticeship for freedom." – Amiri Baraka

The truth is…we are BOLD.

Bold means showing an ability to take risks: both confident and courageous. Tell me that ain't a BLACK character trait!

We are FEARLESS.

Fearless means unafraid: brave, strong willed, having a heart of gold, and being beautiful inside and out. Again, tell me that ain't a BLACK thing!

We are UNAPOLOGETIC!

Unapologetic means not acknowledging or expressing regret. We are THE MOST "OWN IT" kind of people alive. Tell me that ain't a BLACK person!

We are because we choose to be. We fight…and we fight…and much like our ancestors, we don't give up until we get what we came for.

There is a new generation of movers and shakers, fighters and warriors, scholars and teachers, pastors and preachers.

They are Young, Black, and Fearless.

Write it down. What makes young, black, and fearless? I want to hear from you! Email me PERSONALLY at missniasade@gmail.com

---

Do It for Them

TAMIR RICE | TRAYVON MARTIN | MICHAEL BROWN JR. | RENISHA MCBRIDE | AIYANA STANLEY-JONES | REKIA BOYD | NICK THOMAS | ANTHONY HILL | EZELL FORD | KENDRICK JOHNSON | DONTRE HAMILTON | ERIC GARNER | JORDAN DAVIS | JORDAN BAKER | JOHN CRAWFORD III | SEAN BELL | KEVIN DAVIS | TROY ROBINSON | FREDDIE GRAY | TANISHA ANDERSON | AKAI GURLEY | RUMAIN BRISBON | JERAME REID | TONY ROBINSON | PHILLIP WHITE | ERIC HARRIS | WALTER SCOTT | OSCAR GRANT | ERVIN EDWARDS | THADDEUS MCCARROLL | CEDRIC BARTEE | KATHRYN JOHNSTON | RAMARLEY GRAHAM | JOHNATHON FERRELL | MICHAEL ROBINSON | SANDRA BLAND | ANDRE GREEN | DARRIUS STEWART | SAM DUBOSE | KINDRA CHAPMAN | RALKINA JONES | EMMETT TILL | KAJIEME POWELL | DANTE PARKER | TYREE WOODSON | VICTOR WHITE III | YVETTE SMITH | MCKENZIE COCHRAN | MIRIAM CAREY | LARRY

EUGENE JACKSON JR. | DEION FLUDD | KIMANI GRAY | REYNALDO CUEVAS | CHAVIS CARTER | SHANTEL DAVIS | SHARMEL EDWARDS | TAMON ROBINSON | ERVIN JEFFERSON | KENDREC MCDADE | SHEREESE FRANCIS | WENDELL ALLEN | NEHEMIAH DILLARD | DANTE PRICE | RAYMOND ALLEN | SGT. MANUEL LOGGINS JR. | KENNETH CHAMBERLAIN | ALONZO ASHLEY | KENNETH HARDING | RAHEIM BROWN | ARISTON WAITERS | CLEMENTA PINCKNEY | TYWANZA SANDERS | SHARONDA SINGLETON | CYNTHIA HURD | DEPAYNE MIDDLETON-DOCTOR | ETHEL LANCE | SUSIE JACKSON | MYRA THOMPSON | DANIEL SIMMONS SR. | CAINE ROGERS | JAMARION ROBINSON | DE'AUNDRE PHILLIPS | ALTON STERLING | PHILANDO CASTILLE
#RESTINPOWER

"Usually when people are sad, they don't do anything. They just cry over their condition. But when they get angry, they bring about a change." – Malcolm X

I Do It For Them... and Him.

The enemy tried it with me for the longest time. I had focused my activism efforts in fighting for justice of those victims of racial violence. In most cases (if not all) it was White Cop vs. Black Male. I've slept overnight on courthouse steps, organized major movements for justice, made demands in the face of law enforcement, and called out a few elected officials for not holding people accountable, all in the name of JUSTICE for my people. So, you can only imagine how I felt, after putting in all that fight, to have one of the closest people in my life be gunned down by one of our own.

Words can't even begin to express how hurt, pissed off, and broken I felt. How was I supposed to keep fighting when my spirit was torn? I was so angry and couldn't help but think, "Look at what the system did to us!" I was angry at the young man who took my first love's life, but I was even more outraged at the makings of America and how damaging the constructions of this settlement have been on black people. This place is not my home. They robbed my people of our minds! Flawed the education system to prevent from teaching OUR history pre-slavery, so now my people walk around mentally enslaved: killing each other, hurting each other, having to bury one another out of ignorance of the initial plan which was to STEAL, KILL, and DESTROY our race.

Christopher Devon Collins

Gone too soon!!!
We Love you;
until we meet again
R.I.P. Chris.

When Chris was killed, my perspective changed.

I realized that in order to really go hard for the black community,

we have to start at home.

I've heard a few people say that in order for the world to believe

that #BlackLivesMatter, then black lives have to matter to black

people. I didn't care for that comment until I lost a special black

life to the hands of another black life.

I get it now.

That means we have even MORE work to do.

About the Author

Allow me to introduce myself, my name is...N I A.

At 16 - I started putting a price tag to my literary genius.

At 18 - I started my editing business after being granted the chance to edit my mentor's book.

At 20 - I launched my nonprofit organization, Literacy On Purpose, Inc. which was designed to teach and provide opportunities for cultural relevancy to the youth in suburban areas.

At 21 - I wrote and published my first book, *Young Black Fearless: The 7 Step Guide to Activism*, in 10 days.

At 22 - I began assisting other aspiring authors with publishing their books.

At 23 - The **#WriteTheBookChallenge** was created and the **#BlackAuthorsMatter** campaign was born.

Professional Bio

Nia Sadé Akinyemi is a mogul in the making, at only 23 years young. She is a Mother, a College Graduate, Best-Selling Author, Master Editor, Writing Coach, Youth Empowerment Educator, Keynote Speaker, Skilled Vocalist and Social Justice Organizer & Journalist.

Among the rising leaders of the millennial generation, Nia has begun to make a mark throughout Metro Atlanta and across the country. She is known as, "The Literary Revolutionary", as she is CEO & Founder of YBF Publishing. At the top of this year, Nia created the #WriteTheBookChallenge as an effort to promote documentation of the stories and history of people of color. More specifically, Nia has launched a global campaign to encourage, create, and promote more black authors, through Black Authors Matter.

Nia is the Founder & Executive Director of Literacy On Purpose, Inc. Her nonprofit organization aims to educate students in critical areas that lack attention in the public school system setting, such as: Entrepreneurship, Leadership, Service, Cultural History and Diversity. Through this organization, Nia has curated and facilitated several workshops in the literary and social justice arenas, such as: The Writer's Workshop Series, the Teach Write Publish Youth program, and The Blueprint to Activism Project.

Nia has served as the Chairwoman of the Young Adult Council for the NAACP Clayton County Branch. She is a founding member of the Revolutionary Moms Club, an active member of the SisterCARE Alliance where she serves on the Social Justice League, one of the leading organizers of the Clayton and Dekalb County Coalitions for Justice and Police Accountability and the Coalition in Support of Basil Eleby. Additionally, Nia currently represents as the Youth Coordinator of the National Coalition to Combat Police Terrorism.

Nia has recently been named, "The Voice" of the Rising Generation! She is known to "Talk the Talk & Walk the Walk". More importantly, Nia continues to spread the message to her people to write books and document history - because no one can tell our stories, like we can tell our stories.

To Book Nia for speaking engagements, panel discussions, performances, presentations and/or workshops, send an email to: missniasade@gmail.com --- Subject Line: BOOKING

Host The Blueprint to Activism Project or a Revolutionary Writer's Workshop on YOUR campus!

Open to Churches, Community Organizations, High Schools, Colleges & Universities

To register your group for The Blueprint to Activism Project, email: YBFPublishing@gmail.com Subject: Blueprint

.

Figure 1: Nia wraps up a profound lecture, speaking to over 100 teenage girls at Berean Christian Church. .

Figure 2: Nia speaking to students at Georgia Tech.

Figure 3: Nia serving as a Community Activist & Grassroots Organizing Panelist on the "The Uprising Panel" for the 2015 BLOC Conference at New York University.

Figure 4: Nia alongside a few activist friends after a court hearing for a police brutality case in Clayton County, Georgia.

Figure 5: Nia and the children of the NAACP and Revolutionary Moms Club after marching in the Martin Luther King Jr. Parade.